Amara's Adventures

A TRIP TO JACKSONVILLE FLORIDA'S AFRICAN AMERICAN MUSEUMS

> Peace and Love, Friends! I'm Amara. I love learning and discovering new things!

By Nola D Oracle
Illustration by Casielle Santos-Gaerlan

Contents

This special book is dedicated to all the kids who enjoy going on exciting journeys and learning new things along the way! A big shout-out to Florida's African American Museums!

A super special thank you to the fantastic historians in Jacksonville, Florida: Adonnica L. Toler, Saundra Morene, Marsha Dean Phelts, Lloyd Washington, Carol J. Alexander, and Susie Sernaker. You all are truly appreciated for putting in so much time to research and share Florida's African American Culture. Great job!

Peace and Love, Friends! Today, we're going on an exciting adventure to visit some amazing museums in Jacksonville, Florida, that tell us stories about the remarkable African American culture. I'll be your tour guide, so let's go discover and learn together!

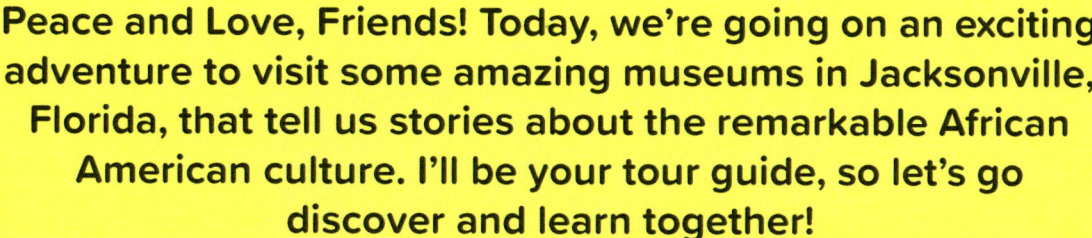

A.L. Lewis American Beach Museum

This is a museum all about the amazing things A.L. Lewis did to help Jacksonville, Florida, and make American Beach awesome!

A.L. Lewis was a really cool person! He was a clever businessman who created the first Afro-American Life Insurance Company to help other African Americans. He worked super hard, and guess what? He became the very first African American millionaire in Jacksonville, Florida.

A.L. Lewis founded a special place called The American Beach, where African Americans could have fun and take vacations together.

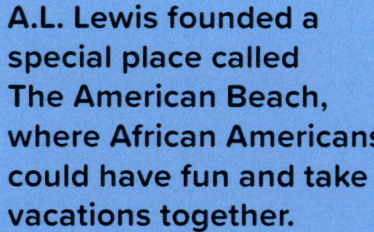

Mavynee Betsch was a special explorer, and she was related to A.L. Lewis, who was her great-grandfather. People called her the beach lady because she loved showing visitors around the beach on fun adventures!

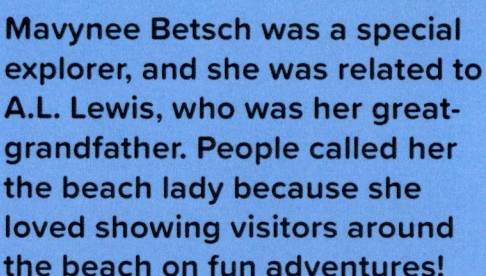

Mavynee was a super heroin who was a defender of American Beach.

When you see colorful butterflies dancing over the sandy dunes at American Beach, remember the remarkable Mavynee!

Mrs. Marsha Dean Phelts was a magical storyteller at the big library in downtown Jacksonville. She wrote a special book called An American Beach for African Americans!

Her book tells stories about how African Americans from all over America would travel to have fun at this special beach. She also shared her happy memories of going on vacations to the amazing American Beach.

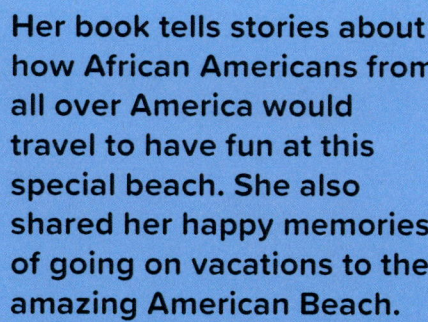

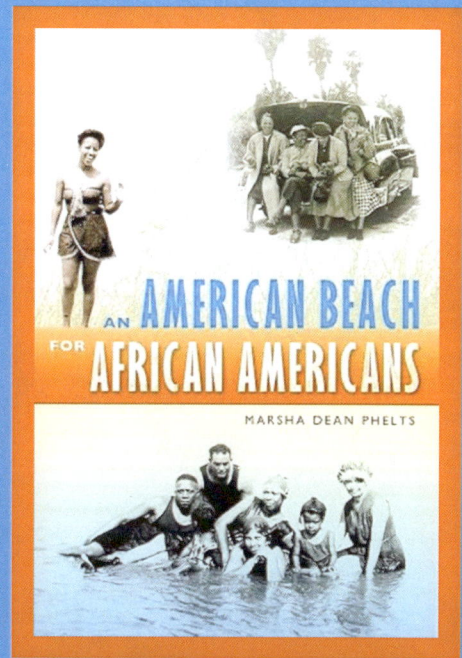

Clara White Center

The Eartha M.M. White Museum is a treasure in the Clara White Mission. Eartha White's mom was Clara White. In this super cool museum, you can discover the exciting story of all the wonderful things Eartha did to make Jacksonville, Florida, a happier and better place.

Eartha White was a wonderful person who helped her community and ran her own business. She was a leader and a friend to many people.

Eartha White got a special invitation to visit the White House from the President, Mr. Nixon! He wanted to say a big thank you for all the wonderful things she did to help her community.

Eartha used to lead African American soldiers from World War II to church, and some of those brave soldiers would stay at the mission during their military travels.

Eartha loved helping children in her community. She believed it was essential that we do all we can, in all the places we can, for all the people we can, while we can.

Durkeeville Museum

At the Durkeeville Museum, you get to hear amazing stories about African Americans who lived in the Durkeeville neighborhood and the big Jacksonville area.

Charlie Hoss Singleton was a super special musician! He was the very first African American who owned the rights to his music and songs.

Alton Yates was a brave adventurer! He was like a superhero for the U.S. Air Force, testing space exploration for the military.

Can you believe he rode a super-fast rocket sled to check how space travel feels on our bodies? In his Jacksonville neighborhood, people called him The Rocket Man!

Jackie Davis played music on a unique keyboard called the Hammond organ. The Hammond Organ was his most favorite instrument.

He made the first jazz album in Jacksonville, Florida. His music made people really happy and inspired other musicians who liked jazz and pop music.

The Durkeeville Museum has an amazing library with lots of fun books for kids, just like you and me!

Ritz Museum

The Ritz Museum is an awesome place that tells exciting stories about remarkable African American trailblazers in Jacksonville, Florida.

James Weldon Johnson was a really cool person! He loved writing stories and poems, and he even helped create a special song called "Lift Every Voice and Sing." James was also a lawyer, which means he knew a lot about laws and rules. He was so talented that he became a big part of the Harlem Renaissance, a time when many people were doing amazing things in art and culture. And guess what? James also had fun playing baseball for the Negro League!

John Rosamond Johnson was a music maker and singer from a special time called the Harlem Renaissance. He made a super important song called the 'Negro National Anthem,' and it's called 'Lift Every Voice and Sing.' John and his brother James Weldon Johnson were like an awesome team because they were both super talented. That's why I call them the dynamic duo' - they were amazing together.

Dr. D. Watson Onley was an architect who built super cool homes.

He was also the first African American to have his very own sawmill in the United States. A sawmill is where trees get turned into flat pieces of wood, and then we use those pieces to build cozy houses!

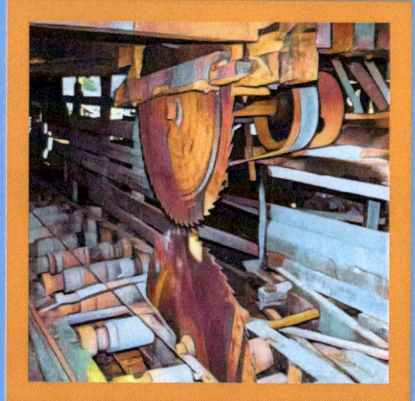

Watson wanted to make sure everyone had happy and healthy smiles, so he decided to become a dentist!

Billy Daniels was a trailblazer! He was the first African American to have his very own TV show. How cool is that?

Stanton was the very first high school for African Americans in Jacksonville, Florida.

The Gullah Geechee people are a special mix of cultures who speak a language called Afro-Creole. Many of them traveled from faraway places in West and Central Africa. Some Gullah Geechee people still live in Jacksonville, Florida. They have their own unique and wonderful community!

The Gullah Geechee people were the first pioneers in growing and creating a cool blue color called indigo blue. They learned this special skill from their families in Africa, which was then shared with the whole world.

Negro League Museum

The Negro Leagues Museum is a unique and exciting place located in J.P. Small Park. This park was built to celebrate and remember James Purcell Small, who was a coach, mentor, and leader in the Durkeeville community.

Andrew Rube Foster was like a superhero in the early 1900s! People called him the father of African American baseball because he was one of the best pitchers. He even invented a cool move called the Curve Ball! Imagine Rube as a baseball wizard making the ball dance in the air- that's how awesome he was!

Toni Stone was a trailblazer in baseball! She was the very first lady to play professional baseball and the first African American woman to join the Negro league. Toni Stone was like a superheroine on thefield, playing as an outfielder for teams like the Indianapolis Clowns, San Francisco Sea Lions, New Orleans Creoles, and the Kansas City Monarchs. She showed everyone that girls and boys can be amazing at baseball!

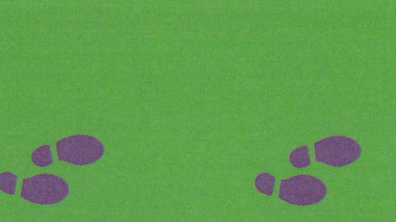

Connie Morgan was a fantastic baseball player, and she was the second woman ever to play professional baseball. She was also the second African American woman to play in a special baseball league called the Negro League. Connie played second base and was really quick, so everyone called her "lightning-fast" because she could run around the bases super fast. She was also a catcher!

Mamie Peanut Johnson was the third woman to play baseball and the third African American woman in the Negro league. Mamie was a pitcher, and she played for the Indianapolis Clowns. Imagine this - Mamie could throw the baseball at a speed of 85 miles per hour with her fastball! She was super talented and helped her team in a big way.

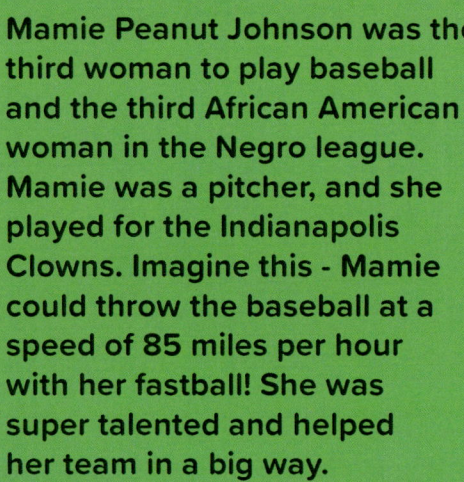

American Beach
Community Center

A.L. LEWIS MUSEUM
PRESERVING THE
LEGACY

CLARA WHITE
CENTER

RITZ

Durkeeville
Historical
Museum